the zen of
mountains and climbing

the zen of
mountains and climbing
wit, wisdom, and inspiration

foreword by Ed Viesturs

edited by Katharine Wroth
illustrations by Kate Quinby

SKIPSTONE

"Come into the mountains, dear friend" reprinted from *Come Into The Mountains, Dear Friend*
by Stephen Schutz and Susan Polis Schutz, published by Blue Mountain Arts. Copyright © 1970,
1971, 1972 by Continental Publications. All rights reserved.

Published by Skipstone, an imprint of The Mountaineers Books
Manufactured in the United States of America

First printing 2009
12 11 10 09   5 4 3 2 1

Compiled and edited by Katherine Wroth
Illustrations by Kate Quinby
Design by Heidi Smets
Cover photograph from istockphoto.com/Brian Prawl

ISBN 978-1-59485-109-4

Library of Congress Cataloging-in-Publication Data
The zen of mountains and climbing : wit, wisdom, and inspiration / foreword by Ed Viesturs ;
edited by Katharine Wroth ; illustrations by Kate Quinby.
      p. cm.
  Includes bibliographical references and index.
  ISBN-13: 978-1-59485-109-4 (alk. paper)
  ISBN-10: 1-59485-109-3 (alk. paper)
  1. Mountaineering—Quotations, maxims, etc. 2. Mountains—Quotations, maxims, etc. I.
Wroth, Katharine. II. Quinby, Kate, ill.
  PN6084.M68Z46 2009
  796.52'2—dc22
                            2008048786

Skipstone books may be purchased for corporate,
educational, or other promotional sales. For
special discounts and information, contact our
Sales Department at 800-553-4453 or
mbooks@mountaineersbooks.org.

Skipstone
1001 SW Klickitat Way, Suite 201
Seattle, Washington 98134
206.223.6303
www.skipstonepress.org
www.mountaineersbooks.org

LIVE LIFE. MAKE RIPPLES.

The mountains are calling and I must go.

—John Muir

listen to the mountain

by Ed Viesturs

They say the third time's the charm, and that was certainly true of
my attempts to reach the summit of Annapurna. For eighteen years,
I had been pursuing the goal of climbing all fourteen of the world's
8,000-meter peaks without supplemental oxygen. Annapurna was the
only one remaining, and I was hungry for it. But I knew the threats
this mountain posed. Twice already I had tried to reach the peak—once
coming within 1,500 feet of my goal—only to walk away because the
conditions were too risky. This time, I had a different strategy: I would
sit at the bottom of the mountain. For as long as it took, I would sit
there and I would listen. I would let the mountain tell me whether I
should go up or go home.

I listened, I looked, and this time the mountain seemed welcoming,
not dangerous. The weather was clear. No avalanches threatened. As
my partner and I made our way up the steeper sections, the ice cliffs
poised above us didn't fall. Maybe, I thought, this was karma coming
back around. It certainly felt like someone was watching over us.

We made it to the top on that climb, and as I stood on the
summit—a place I had thought I might never reach—it was a
dream-come-true moment.

I truly believe our success on Annapurna had to do with taking time
to listen to the mountain, and I believe that's the key to a good climb
no matter where you are. A lot of people look at climbers as foolish,

as risk-takers—and some are, there's no doubt. But attaining a summit does not have to be a near-death experience. If you approach your mountain or your rock face in a humble, respectful way, if you don't go out to conquer it, if you let it decide for you when to go and when not to go, you will have a successful climb. You can't have zero risk in the mountains, but you can reduce the risks by being smart.

Being smart also means focusing on the journey, on the reason you're out there in the first place, and not just on the summit. Climbing is about being with friends; it's about enjoying amazing and wild places; it's about testing yourself physically, emotionally, and mentally. A lot of people want instant gratification, but you've got to take things one step at a time. Mountaineering is about patience. It's about, as a friend likes to say, "paying the currency of toil." You've got to work hard, and you've got to make smart choices.

I've tried to practice this philosophy—working hard, making smart choices, and enjoying the journey—since my very first climb. Growing up in Illinois, I read the story of the first ascent of Annapurna, and was immediately hooked. I didn't know then the role Annapurna would play in my life, but I knew that mountains and climbing were for me. So I moved to Washington State to go to college and to be among mountains. In 1977, I climbed my first peak: Mount St. Helens. Standing at the top, I looked around and thought, "This is it. This experience is exactly what I dreamed it would be."

More than thirty years later, I've had the pleasure of seeing that type of joy dawn on the faces of many other first-timers. For years, I guided trips on Mount Rainier, and over the course of 200 ascents of my "backyard mountain" it's been incredible to witness the way people see the wonders around them, the energy they feel. It gives me great energy in return.

I think all climbers—whether they're mountaineers or rock jocks—share a similar spirit. There's a love of wild places, a great satisfaction in completing a climb, and an addiction of sorts that keeps you coming back to the mountains again and again. The quotations collected here give a glimpse of the motivations climbers feel, the risks they're willing to take, the joy and pain they experience—and, yes, even the peace they achieve.

When I finally reached the summit of Annapurna, I felt a mix of such emotions: happiness at having accomplished my goal, but sadness that my eighteen-year effort was over; exhaustion, but elation; and underlying it all, simple awe at standing in such a place. I believe we all have our own Annapurnas in our lives, and I encourage you to keep reaching for yours, whatever it may be. Just remember to savor the journey—and remember to listen.

why we climb

Whether it's for sheer enjoyment or a career, whether motivated by curiosity or compulsion, every mountaineer and rock climber has a reason to head for the hills.

The plethora of writing about mountains and the people who climb them is rife with that enduring question: Why?

—Jonathan Waterman

He could not have given the reason, but the mountain tormented him, beckoned him, held an answer to something he wanted. It was so pure, so austere.

—Norman Mailer

The quest for the unknown is my draw to the mountains.

—Conrad Anker

Climbing is like a religion for me. I love being outside, I love exercising, and I love sharing it with my kids.

—Jacinda Hunter

I feel that climbing is a part of who I am. It's my way of life. It's my way of expressing myself. My way of being in the world.

—Chris Sharma

You must ascend a mountain to learn your relation to matter, and so to your own body, for it is at home there, though you are not.

—Henry David Thoreau

Climbing needs no justification, no more than does watching a sunrise, or listening to a great symphony, or falling in love ... Rock and ice and wind and the great blue canopy of the sky are not all that [a climber] finds upon the mountaintops. He discovers things about his own body and mind he had almost forgotten ... He finds the divine harmony and simplicity of the natural world, and himself alive in it, a part of it.

—James Ramsey Ullman

I have to climb. It's just a cross I have to bear.

—Aly Dorey

If one should ask me what "use" there was in climbing, or attempting to climb the world's highest peak, I would be compelled to answer "none." There is no scientific end to be served; simply the gratification of the impulse of achievement, the indomitable desire to see what lies beyond that ever beats within the heart of man.

—George Mallory

A born climber's appetite for climbing is hard to satisfy; when it comes upon him he is like a starving man with a feast before him; he may have other business on hand, but it must wait.

—Mark Twain

That so many view climbing as "a sport" shows me they are less focused on the deeper mysteries, the values of beauty, tenderness, and friendship, the incredible communication it is possible for us to have with nature, in all its variety. When we compete, we try to defeat someone else and to elevate ourselves. That's the most mundane of reasons to climb.

—Pat Ament

The professional aspects of [climbing] do add stress, but it is definitely better than a desk job and we make sure to keep that perspective.

—Tommy Caldwell and Beth Rodden

Climbing is about the journey up the face. It can take seconds, minutes, days or years. If you ask, "Why climb rocks?," it's all about the movement and the flow, calculating the most efficient way to use only what the rock offers to move upwards. "Why go climbing?" is a bigger question; sometimes the actual climbing is only a fraction of the experience. Friendships, travel, scenery—so many ingredients are all bound together by climbing itself.

—Steve McClure

You know, if you see a mountain, and you think, "My God, I'm never gonna climb over that mountain," that's all the more reason to climb over that mountain.

—Kate Winslet

The influence of fine scenery, the presence of mountains, appeases our irritations and elevates our friendships.

—Ralph Waldo Emerson

When you climb all worries in the world disappear. You are so present and focused on what you are doing, and flow[ing] smoothly, and being as efficient as you can, and I love that. I've got a really noisy head and it just quiets [the] thing down for me.

—Jack Osbourne

Climbing is unadulterated hard labor. The only real pleasure is the satisfaction of going where no man has been before and where few can follow.

—Annie Smith Peck

I wasn't interested in mountains. If he [Bradford Washburn] had been a sailor, I would have gone sailing.

—Barbara Washburn

Separate from the pleasure of your company, I don't much care if I never see another mountain in my life.

—Charles Lamb to William Wordsworth

I climbed Everest so you wouldn't have to.

—Tenzing Norgay to his son

I long for the high places—they are so clean and pure and untouched.

—Ansel Adams

Because it is there.

—George Mallory, in explanation for attempting to climb Everest

where we climb

From the beginning of time, mountains have been a source of mystery and magnificence, not only to those who climb them, but to those who simply admire them from afar.

We never tire of looking at each other,
Only the mountain and I.

—Li Po

After having studied this mountain in countless photographs, I thought I'd be prepared for this first sighting. But I wasn't. After a few minutes, a feeling of warmth and contentment came over me and I marveled at how something as nonorganic as a mountain can move one so deeply.

—Jochen Hemmleb, upon first seeing Everest

Great things are done when men and mountains meet;
This is not done by jostling in the street.

—William Blake

The mountains ... are a passive mystery, the oldest of all. Theirs is the one simple mystery of creation from nothing, of matter itself, anything at all, the given. Mountains are giant, restful, absorbent. You can heave your spirit into a mountain and the mountain will keep it, folded, and not throw it back as some creeks will. The creeks are the world with all its stimulus and beauty; I live there. But the mountains are home.

—Annie Dillard

Two voices are there: one is of the Sea,
One of the Mountains; each a mighty Voice ...

—William Wordsworth

In the mountains, worldly attachments are left behind, and in the absence of material distractions, we are opened up to spiritual thought. When we look out at the ocean or gaze at the sky and the clouds, or even the rock wall of a mountain, it is difficult for our minds to form labels. What is it really that we are looking at? There is no real thing there—just color and shape. And when we stop attaching labels to what we see, a sense of quietness flows in to fill the gap, bringing us a step closer to the understanding of emptiness.

—Jamling Norgay

Mountains are Earth's undecaying monuments.

—Nathaniel Hawthorne

I can't do with mountains at close quarters—they are always in the way, and they are so stupid, never moving and never doing anything but obtrude themselves.

—D.H. Lawrence

The ordinary man looking at a mountain is like an illiterate person confronted with a Greek manuscript.

—Aleister Crowley

The mountains can be reached in all seasons. They offer a fighting challenge to heart, soul and mind, both in summer and winter. If throughout time the youth of the nation accept the challenge the mountains offer, they will keep alive in our people the spirit of adventure.

—William O. Douglas

What would be ugly in a garden constitutes beauty in
a mountain.

—Victor Hugo

After climbing a great hill, one only finds that there are many more hills to climb. I have taken a moment here to rest, to steal a view of the glorious vista that surrounds me, to look back on the distance I have come. But I can rest only for a moment, for with freedom comes responsibilities, and I dare not linger, for my long walk is not yet ended.

—Nelson Mandela

If one does not climb tall mountains, one cannot view
the plains.

—Chinese proverb

... give me the islands of the upper air,
all mountains
and the towering mountain trees.

—Hilda Doolittle

The Buddha, the Godhead, resides quite as comfortably in the circuits of a digital computer or the gears of a cycle transmission as he does at the top of a mountain or in the petals of a flower.

—Robert M. Pirsig

Mountains are to the rest of the body of the earth, what violent muscular action is to the body of man. The muscles and tendons of its anatomy are, in the mountain, brought out with force and convulsive energy, full of expression, passion, and strength.

—John Ruskin

If I wished to see a mountain or other scenery under the most favorable auspices, I would go to it in foul weather, so as to be there when it cleared up; we are then in the most suitable mood, and nature is most fresh and inspiring. There is no serenity so fair as that which is just established in a tearful eye.

—Henry David Thoreau

Today is your day!
Your mountain is waiting.
So … get on your way.

—Dr. Seuss

In the mountains, there you feel free.

—T.S. Eliot

And over all the sky—the sky! far, far out of reach,
studded, breaking out, the eternal stars.

—Walt Whitman

ups and downs

There's no telling what will happen during the course of navigating a rocky trail or a sheer face, but one thing is certain: climbers must be flexible, in both body and spirit.

Climbers need only very basic things: good food and water, and we don't have many demands for where we sleep. I mean, sometimes we sleep on rock or in the air. You go with the flow.

—Lynn Hill

Climbing is physical. It involves movement, involves a connection with nature that is intimate. You have to get to know nature and yourself … you must get to know about strength and endurance, you must get to know about figuring it out with your mind. You can't make a move on rock without thinking it out first; then the physical movement, the emotions. It requires great focus: mental, physical, emotional, and spiritual.

—Tom Frost

[My] relaxed attitude to climbing meant I enjoyed it and never felt pressure to be good or achieve too much. I think when people put too much pressure on themselves it can backfire.

—Joanna George

Don't take climbing too seriously that you become a slave to it. I saw people so plugged into climbing that they couldn't get their minds around anything else. By the time they got out of the car to climb, they were so worked up—so intense about climbing—that they couldn't enjoy the experience. I think that holds a lot of people back. I think those people should re-learn how to just relax, and enjoy what they are doing.

—Jim Holloway

[As] I sat by myself and looked over the scenery the sun came out, and the wind died down a little. Suddenly I felt completely calm. I knew without a doubt that I could do the route, and that this was the moment. When I led the route, everything fell into place. The moves flowed and I felt completely in control all the way up. It was the most amazing experience for me. My mind overcame all the fear and doubt and … my body [moved] instinctively into the perfect positions.

—Lisa Rands

I've been up the mountain and I had a choice.
Should I come down? So I came down. God said,
"Okay, you've been up on the mountain, now you
go down. You're on your own, free. Check in later,
but now you're on your own."

—Bob Dylan

Climbing is about working with nature and what's going on around you, the weather, the rock. It's not about conquering.

—Nancy Feagin

You've got to know when to turn around.

—John Roskelley

It's not advisable to drink too much strong liquors while climbing in the Alps. If, however, you are going to fall over a cliff, it's advisable to be thoroughly intoxicated when you do so.

—Attributed to an English alpinist

Every now and again you have 'a moment' when everything comes together; the whole world around you fits together perfectly. I can climb for a whole year for just a few instances of this. They stay with me forever afterwards.

—Steve McClure

To do good is like ascending a mountain; to do evil as easy as following an avalanche.

—Chinese proverb

A few hours' mountain climbing turns a rogue and a saint into two roughly equal creatures. Weariness is the shortest path to equality and fraternity—and liberty is finally added by sleep.

—Friedrich Nietzsche

Technique and ability alone do not get you to the top, it is the willpower that is the most important. This willpower you cannot buy with money or be given by others—it rises from your heart.

—Junko Tabei

While it helps, of course, to have tough muscles, the prizefighter would not necessarily make a fine Dolomite climber. But the ballet dancer might.

—Miriam Underhill

Come into the mountains, dear friend
Leave society and take no one with you
But your true self
Get close to nature
Your everyday games will be insignificant
Notice the clouds spontaneously forming patterns
And try to do that with your life.

—Susan Polis Schutz

It doesn't seem so much to climb a mountain
You've worked around the foot of all your life.

—Robert Frost

In mountains, where personality counts before everything, men are forced back upon their elemental selves; they become very different beings from their drawingroom semblances, and unless they allow for this in the adjustment of their relations on the hills, they can achieve only the mediocrity of performance, the barrenness in results, or the complete breakdown which are the common fate of all ill-constituted parties, for exploration, for mountaineering, for warfare, or for any other active adventure that depends for its success upon effective combination.

—Geoffrey Winthrop Young

When you're high on a mountain you cannot be anything but what you are.

—Reinhold Messner

risk among
the rocks

Most climbers pursue their passion
despite the very real risks involved—
or is it because of those risks? In
climbing, fear and fulfillment go
hand in hand.

There is probably no pleasure equal to the pleasure of climbing a dangerous Alp; but it is a pleasure which is confined strictly to people who can find pleasure in it.

—Mark Twain

The combination of controlling every position of my body and of forcing my mind to shut out the ever-present urge to submit to the very real fear of falling created an interesting result: a feeling that I was simultaneously acutely aware of both everything and nothing.

—Lynn Hill

The climb had released a tide of emotions and insights. I'd already discovered that, once you've survived intense situations like this, you immediately find yourself becoming determined not to repeat them … But the horrors fade. Soon there is something new. You never finish.

—Robert Schauer, on surviving a blizzard in the Karakoram

Unless it feels impossible, it's just a sport. If it's
impossible, then it's not a sport—it's internal
adventure and an external adventure. When the
internal and external adventure plaque together
beautifully, there is a spark of recognition between the
invisible and the visible, which sets your heart alive.

—Johnny Dawes

When climbing, the presence of mind that one needs in dangerous situations makes one naturally undistracted, and that undistractedness is what generates awareness and a feeling of being completely alive. Every action becomes meaningful because each movement is a matter of life and death.

—Jamling Norgay

Sooner or later … you are going to be looking at
God saying, "We're going to be lucky if we get out
of here." Your life is going to be in front of you and
then you are going to realize that you'd rather be
grocery shopping.

—Ed Barry

At this altitude the boundaries between life and death are fluid.

—Peter Habeler

Many climbers experience the undeniable and powerful dreams of plunging endlessly through space, of blood rinsing your face with the smell of copper, of running but not moving in front of a monster avalanche, or any of a hundred deaths so textured and memorable that they give pause to even our best climbs.

—Jonathan Waterman

I once heard someone define Himalayan climbing as the 'art of suffering.' I understand the suffering part, but I'm not sure I fully grasp the artistic challenge. Unless he meant the sort of artistic talent is takes to imagine that you are actually sleeping in a tent that is perched on a 50-degree angle with a fatal drop directly below.

—Heidi Howkins

I am afraid if there is anything to be afraid of. A
precipice cannot hurt you. Lions and tigers can.
The streets of New York I consider more dangerous
than the Matterhorn to a thoroughly competent and
careful climber.

—Annie Smith Peck

Climbing is the lazy man's way to enlightenment. It forces you to pay attention, because if you don't, you won't succeed, which is minor—or you may get hurt, which is major. Instead of years of meditation, you have this activity that forces you to relax and monitor your breathing and tread that line between living and dying. When you climb, you always are confronted with the edge. Hey, if it was just like climbing a ladder, we all would have quit a long time ago.

—Duncan Ferguson

Remember not to have a fatal accident, because the community will think climbing is a dangerous thing, your friends will be bummed … and you'll be dead.

—Kitty Calhoun

I once heard a man professing religion say it was a sin to climb, because it was to risk the sacred gift of life God gave us. Another person, in my eyes far more spiritual, told me it would be a sin not to climb, for climbing was, in his eyes, God-given.

—Pat Ament

If the conquest of a great peak brings moments of exultation and bliss, which in the monotonous, materialistic existence of modern times nothing else can approach, it also presents great dangers. It is not the goal of grand alpinism to face peril, but it is one of the tests one must undergo to deserve the joy of rising for an instant above the state of crawling grubs.

—Lionel Terray

Q: What's the difference between a bad golfer and
    a bad climber ?
A: A bad golfer sounds like this: "Whack … Damn!"
    A bad climber sounds like this: "Damn … Whack!"

—Anonymous

Soloing is serious business, because you can
be seriously dead.

—John Bachar

Climbing is mostly very exhilarating because
you're potentially dead—but I never liked the
cheap thrill of it.

—Jim Erickson

By this point we knew if they didn't reach us then, we had little chance of surviving. We didn't need to talk about it. You just need to look into someone's eyes and you know they understand the seriousness of the situation as well as you do. It was such a relief when they finally reached us.

—Rachel Kelsey, after being rescued in the Swiss Alps

Getting to the summit is optional. Getting down is
mandatory. The summit of a mountain is not where
I want to die.

—Ed Viesturs

There have been joys too great to be described in words, and there have been griefs upon which I have not dared to dwell, and with these in mind I say, climb if you will, but remember that courage and strength are naught without prudence, and that a momentary negligence may destroy the happiness of a lifetime. Do nothing in haste, look well to each step, and from the beginning think what may be the end.

—Edward Whymper

"We'll make it."

"I don't think so. But we shall continue with style."

—Exchange between Dr. Jonathan Hemlock and
Anderl Meyer in the movie *The Eiger Sanction* (1975)

life at the top

If the summit is your goal, little else equals
the satisfaction of getting there. Despite
aching muscles and weary mind, reaching
the top offers an undeniable jolt to the spirit.

Now away we go toward the topmost mountains. Many still, small voices, as well as the noon thunder, are calling, 'Come higher.' Farewell, blessed dell, woods, gardens, streams, birds, squirrels, lizards, and a thousand others. Farewell, farewell.

—John Muir

I think we go up so we can come back down again. This coming down is a very strong experience. You come back from an inhuman place. We are not made for it, this loneliness and cold. When you come back you feel reborn, you have a new chance. The experience is so strong you want to have it again and again, but you have to suffer for it. It's addictive.

—Reinhold Messner

You can't see the entire world from the top of Everest …
The view from there only reminds you how big the world is
and how much more there is to see and learn.

—Tenzing Norgay

When you get to the top of K2, there's nowhere left to go. You've succeeded against the world's toughest mountain. There is the cessation of passion, of the desire to move forever upwards. There is emptiness, and the closure of a circle. You are back where you started. And you're at peace.

—Heidi Howkins

Man can climb to the highest summits; but he cannot dwell there long.

—George Bernard Shaw

Behind one high mountain lies yet a higher one.

—Chinese proverb

I have been in Sorrow's kitchen and licked out all the pots. Then I have stood on the peaky mountain wrapped in rainbows, with a harp and a sword in my hands.

—Zora Neale Hurston

Night's candles are burnt out, and jocund day
Stands tiptoe on the misty mountain tops.

—Shakespeare (*Romeo and Juliet*)

We knocked the bastard off.

—Edmund Hillary, on completing the first
successful ascent of Everest

Never measure the height of a mountain until you have reached the top.

—Dag Hammarskjöld

[It] always unsettled me, this moment of reaching the summit, this sudden stillness and quiet after the storm, which gave me time to wonder at what I was doing and sense a niggling doubt that perhaps I was inexorably losing control—was I here purely for pleasure or was it egotism? Did I really want to come back for more? But these moments were also good times, and I knew that the feelings would pass. Then I could excuse them as morbid pessimistic fears that had no sound basis.

—Joe Simpson

Making it to the top isn't about a final sprint; it's about maintaining your rhythm—even if that rhythm is five breaths for every one step. That kind of focus means that you're more likely to have the energy to deal with unforeseen challenges—and less likely to lose sight of why you're climbing the mountain in the first place.

—Arlene Blum

There [are] a lot of people that maybe focus too much on getting to the top. They just want to get to the top and have that success, which is too bad, because so much of it takes place in the process of working on it. That's the whole life of it.

—Chris Sharma

Achieving the summit of a mountain was tangible,
immutable, concrete. The incumbent hazards lent the
activity a seriousness of purpose that was sorely missing
from the rest of my life. I thrilled in the fresh perspective
that came from tipping the ordinary plane of existence
on end.

—Jon Krakauer

The summit provides a reason for turning back and climbing down, but rarely, in my experience, a climax. For me the emotional peak had been when we rose from the ocean of cloud when, emerging from the storm, we were presented with the gift of a chance …

It would have been good to linger on the top. To soak up that beautiful, enchanted place in the golden light and watch the sun sink into the sea of boiling cloud that flowed, in a slow, interminable current, out of Asia and washed upon the mountain island, the westernmost bastion of the Himalaya.

—Roger Mear, on a climb of Nanga Parbat

You cannot always stay on the summits. You have to come down again … So what's the point? Only this: what is above knows what is below, what is below does not know what is above.

—René Daumal

Life for two weeks on the mountaintops would show up many things about life during the other fifty weeks down below.

—Benton MacKaye

The ascent is over. But it lives with us forever. Five days … and a moment of grace.

—Kurt Diemberger, on summiting Mont Blanc

When you reach the top, keep climbing.

—Zen proverb